Sell It Online

How to Make Money Selling on eBay, Amazon, Fiverr, & Etsy

Copyright © 2014 / 2022 by Nick Vulich

Table of Contents

Getting Started 1

Sell it on eBay 14

Sell it on Amazon 46

Sell it on Etsy 62

Kindle Book Marketing 74

Blogging 96

Online Courses & Coaching 109

What's next? 119

Getting Started

Everybody dreams about making money online.

Who wouldn't want a job where you can work at home in your jammies or underwear? A job where you don't have bosses riding your rear end telling you what to do, how to do it, or how soon to do it?

Selling online can be all of that and more.

Contrary to popular belief, it's not easy. No. You won't have the boss riding your tail telling you what to do, but you will find yourself working harder than you ever did at your day job.

You will find yourself short on cash, especially when you start.

Just because you decide to hang your shingle out on eBay, Amazon, or any other online site, doesn't mean buyers will magically flock to your items and shower you with cash.

Like anything else, selling products or services online takes time.

Anyone can go online, list a few items, and score a few quick sales. However, the key to being a successful online seller is duplicating this process, day in and day out, month after month.

This means you need to:

- Discover a stream of products you can sell over and over again.
- Build a steady and satisfied client base.
- Find a niche that sets your business apart.
- Stay one step ahead of your customers, and offer products they want before they even know they want them.
- Understand your numbers. Too many online sellers believe raking in large sums of money means making a profit. But, unfortunately, many of them discover too late their earnings are eaten up by fees and expenses they weren't aware of.

So, Where Do You Start?

One of the first things you need to do is decide what you want to sell.

Many first-time sellers try to sell everything but the kitchen sink. But unfortunately, this strategy often doesn't work for them because, like any other business, online businesses rely heavily upon repeat buyers. And, it's hard to attract repeat buyers if you're selling old magazines one day, used tools another day, and toys another day.

To build a successful online business that will grow and thrive over the long haul, you need to pick a profitable niche and consistently offer products or services your buyers want and are willing to pay for.

Let me repeat: **Pick a profitable niche** and consistently offer products and services **your buyers want** and **are willing to pay for**.

Are you going to offer a product or a service?

What you choose to sell will determine which platforms you should sell on.

For the purpose of this book, we're going to look at three basic types of offers:

1) Products
2) Crafts
3) Services

Products are tangible items. Some examples are books, clothes, electronics, collectibles, and toys.

Crafts are handmade either by you or by someone else. Examples include dolls, decorator light switches, floral arrangements, quilts, and custom-made lingerie.

Services can be a combination of products and intangible items. Examples of services include product reviews, logo design, website design, tarot or psychic readings, custom videos, and similar items.

Products are better suited to selling on eBay, Amazon, eBid, eCRATER, and bidStart because buyers come to these places looking for tangible products. Buyers are on eBay and Amazon shopping for things.

Crafts can be sold on most online platforms. Your best bet is probably Etsy because it is a marketplace designed exclusively for crafts and vintage items. That's not to say craft items won't sell on eBay or Amazon. Etsy is a site designed to cater to Craft enthusiasts. The odds are it will be your best market for them, but you need to test drive all three sites to determine which marketplace works the best for what you're selling.

If you're unsure whether your item will sell on one marketplace or another, run some test listings to help you decide. The worst that can happen is your item won't sell.

If you sell services, you definitely want to be on Fiverr.

Fiverr is a marketplace where buyers offer their services for five bucks. Let me warn you. It's just crazy what some of these sellers are willing to do for $5.00. A small sample of the services offered on Fiverr includes logo design, blog writing, custom videos, product reviews, book reviews, and music videos.

eBay is another solid choice for selling services. Compared to Fiverr, you should command a higher price for your work, but the demand for services isn't as high as it is on Fiverr, so you will get less work. Services I see thriving on eBay include logo design, webpage design, eBay store design, and Facebook headers.

A good choice for service providers would probably be to offer your complete services on eBay and offer an abbreviated version of them on Fiverr to test the waters. We will go into this in much more detail later in this book.

Building Your Clientele

To be an online seller for the long haul, you must build a steady stream of repeat buyers.

How do you develop repeat buyers?

The simple answer is:

- Offer unique products buyers can't find anywhere else.
- Give great customer service.
- Specialize (be an expert) in the products you sell.

With that said, how do you do these three things?

The fact is they all sort of blend together. People who recognize you as an expert in your product line feel good about spending their money with you. They will contact you with questions regarding authenticity, history, and value. At the same time, many will offer to sell you items or be open to buying the item they are inquiring about.

Customer service means promptly answering buyer questions, not just with a yes or a no, but really answering their questions and telling them more than they asked.

Customer service means going out of your way to professionally pack and ship your items. Don't just toss them into a box or envelope. Carefully wrap everything you send. Include instructions for the care and handling of the things you sell. If your item requires installation, include detailed information about installing it. Better yet, add links to an installation video, or embed it within your item description page.

Another way to position yourself as an expert is to write books and articles on your subject matter.

Let's say you sell pre-1950s sports cards and memorabilia. You could position yourself as a subject matter expert by writing short Kindle books on different card sets, how to grade cards, and when to use a professional grading service.

Another idea here would be to make a print book using Create Space. Then, for as little as $2.17 per copy, you can print a 100-page book that is professionally bound.

If you show your print book on every item description page and mention you are the author, that's even better. You will build instant credibility with your buyers. In addition, if you sell high-dollar value items, you may want to include a copy for free with every qualifying sale.

This idea will also work for crafters and service providers and help you stand out from your competition.

How do you get more items to sell?

How you find inventory depends upon what you sell.

You will purchase most of your inventory through wholesalers if you sell new items like electronics, books, or clothes. Most wholesalers require you to have a resale permit. Many of them also want to know a little more about your business and how you plan to sell the items you purchase. They won't sell to you if you mention you sell on eBay or Amazon. So you need to develop a game plan to approach wholesalers.

If you sell collectibles, you have a couple of options.

Many hobbies have collectibles shows. Smart dealers grab a table or two at these events to purchase inventory. This works exceptionally well if you advertise beforehand that you will be there armed with cash and ready to buy. Other dealers advertise in enthusiast magazines and local newspapers.

If you sell used clothing—yard sales and estate sales are excellent ways to pick up inventory on the cheap. In addition, the Salvation Army Store, Good Will, and other thrift stores typically have a great selection of new and gently used clothes you can resell at a good profit.

If you shop thrift stores, yard sales, or estate sales, check out *9 Easy Ways to Start Making Money on eBay in 72 Hours or Less* by Michelle Angell. She gives a great breakdown on approaching each type of sale and how to bargain for the best deals.

I've found many great items I can resell at Target, Wal-Mart, TJ Maxx, and Kohls's. Many sellers work this strategy and buy seasonal closeouts and hold them until the start of next year's season when they can sell them for higher prices.

If you purchase most of your items during closeout sales at local retailers, check out *Barcode Booty* by Steve Weber. Steve is an expert in online selling. He talks about how online sellers can find hot-selling products at local closeout sales using barcode scanners, cell phones, or a PDA.

The idea behind using scanning software makes good sense. Your phone or PDA is attached to the Amazon catalog. So when you scan a barcode, it gives you the item's product rank and selling price on Amazon. This way, you can pick the products that sell right there while you're in the store looking at them. People also use these scanners at used bookstores and library book sales to help select the few gems that will make them money.

If you want to try a barcode scanner application on the cheap, download the Price Check Android App on Amazon. There is also an iPhone app available.

Amazon designed Price Check to be a comparison shopping tool for their customers to use when they are in stores, but it works just as well to check Amazon's values to see if you can score a profit. The app lets you scan barcodes, type in the item name or UPC, speak the product name using voice recognition, or snap a picture and let Amazon's photo recognition software match it up. Then, within a few seconds, it tells you what the item is currently selling for on Amazon.

Give it a try the next time you're shopping the closeout aisles. See what you think!

Another sourcing idea that has always worked for me is scouring eBay for items I can resell. This works because so many sellers have no idea what they are selling, and many of them are just plain lazy (they don't describe what they're selling well, or they only include one picture when five or six would sell the item).

Try it once. Pick a few categories and spend fifteen or twenty minutes daily searching for items you think are underpriced or listed poorly. You should easily locate five to ten things you can resell for a sweet profit.

Another idea I borrowed from Frank on the American Pickers is bundling products to increase sales. Bundling can work with just about any product.

Typically paperback books are slow sellers on eBay, but if you can pick up five or six books in a series by the same author and bundle them, this will often catch a reader's eye. Or how about if you grouped four or five books on dieting and weight loss or online selling and listed them at a premium price.

The same thing works with clothing. Again, slow-selling items do well when you bundle them into complete outfits.

Think of yourself as a value-added reseller when you bundle items, and you will do well. Bundles can make your articles stand out if you price them competitively.

After you've been at it for a while, you will be able to develop a buying and merchandising strategy that works well for your online business.

You need to know your numbers

The worst thing that can happen is to go full blast into online selling, thinking you're making beau-coups bucks because money keeps pouring into your PayPal account, only to discover later that it isn't so. But, unfortunately, this happens way too often.

You need to know your numbers to make a profit in any business.

There is a vast difference between money coming in and making a profit. To make a profit, you need to make enough money to cover all your expenses plus the cost of the items you sell. Anything left over after covering your expenses is profit.

Sounds easy, doesn't it?

Here are just a few of the expenses you're going to have in any online venture:

- Cost of the goods you are selling
- eBay fees (Store fee, listing fees, final value fees, extras)
- Amazon fees (ProMerchant fee, selling fees, per item fees)
- Fiverr fees ($1.08 from every item sold goes to Fiverr and PayPal – you keep $3.92 of every $5.00 you take in)

- Etsy fees (.20 for every item listed, 3.5% of the selling price, and a payment processing fee of 3% plus .25 per transaction)
- Internet provider fees
- PayPal or merchant account processing fees
- Packing supplies (boxes, envelopes, peanuts, bubble wrap)
- Postage (insurance, shipping, tracking fees)
- Collateral services (Auctiva, Vendio, Ink Frog – any similar tools you use to enhance listings or for picture storage)
- Advertising (Google or Amazon pay-per-click ads)
- Automobile expenses (gas, mileage – for going to the post office, shopping for supplies, or purchasing inventory)
- Phone, fax, computer, scanner, digital camera
- Home office expenses (desk, chair, and expenses for remodeling your office)
- Home-related bills (if you claim the home office deduction, you can also deduct the portion of utilities, sewer, trash, and other home-related expenses)

These expenses add up quickly. If you don't keep careful track of them, you can easily fool yourself into thinking you're making a profit when you're losing your ass.

Some sellers record expenses with Excel or Quick Books. Whatever method you use to track your income, make sure you save your receipts and record your sales.

At the end of the year, you are required to report your online income to the IRS.

The government has imposed mandatory reporting requirements upon PayPal to keep everyone honest. For example, if you receive more than $20,000 in payments (It's changing to $600 in 2022), PayPal must report it to the IRS on Form 1099-K.

To view your form 1099-K, sign into your PayPal Account, and hover your pointer over the **history** tab, which will bring up a drop-down menu. Next, you want to click on **tax documents**, allowing you to view a PDF file of your 1099-K if one was generated for you.

You are not required to submit the PayPal 1099-K with your income tax filing, but you should be sure you are reporting at least as much income as is shown on it. You can be sure the IRS matches them up and looks closely at your 1099-K and the income you report on your tax return.

Sell it on eBay

It's estimated that nearly 1,000,000 people in the United States currently make a full-time or part-time income selling on eBay.

These are the people we all envy who work from home in their jammies and underwear.

Get Started

Getting started selling on eBay is about as easy as it gets. The folks at eBay offer many great tutorials, and the sell-your-item form walks you through a lot of the information you need along the way.

You need to register for an eBay account to begin selling if you don't already have one. At the same time, you need to sign up for eBay's managed payments. They collect payments from buyers and deposit the proceeds in your account two to three days later.

eBay offers casual sellers fifty free auction listings every month. I would suggest you start here and list a few items. This way, you can test the waters to make sure you're comfortable selling on eBay before you invest a lot of time or money into something you might not like.

Selling on eBay can be fun, but it's not for everyone. So test the waters first before you jump in with both guns blazing.

Be a buyer first, then a seller

If you've never bought anything on eBay, it will be hard for you to be a good seller.

I say this because it's a lot easier to be a good seller once you understand why and how people buy stuff on eBay.

People shop on eBay for many different reasons. Some people shop on eBay because they're looking for items on the cheap. They want to wear designer clothes, but they can't afford to buy them new.

Collectors scour eBay listings every day, looking for that rare missing piece they want to add to their collection. These are the people sellers love to bid on their auctions because they get lost in their desire to have the item and fuel a bidding frenzy.

Other people buy on eBay because they don't like shopping at stores. They're tired of pushy salespeople, crowded parking lots, and stores that run out of stock on the items they want. Shopping on eBay saves people time and frustration.

Many people like the excitement. For them buying on eBay is like spending a day at the casino. They like to bid on items and win things at auction. These people are after the rush of excitement and the thrill of winning.

It would help if you bought a few things first and experienced some of these emotions before you started to sell on eBay. But, in the long run, it will help you better understand what your buyers want and why they are buying from you.

Another reason you must be a buyer first is to rack up some good feedback before selling.

One of the great things about eBay is that buyers and sellers can rate each transaction they participate in and grade each other on a scale of one to five. Sellers strive for five-star feedback because it offers social proof they are a reliable seller who delivers a great buying experience.

People are going to be leery of buying from you if you hang your shingle out there and start trying to sell with a big old zero for your feedback rating. That zero will make most people steer clear of you because you are an unknown quantity. This is especially true if you sell higher-priced items or items where lots of sellers with awesome feedback offer the same thing for sale.

The easiest way around this is to buy a few things. Then, pay quickly, leave excellent feedback for your seller, and wait to receive feedback for your purchases.

My suggestion is to buy ten or fifteen small items over a week. Then, after you have ten five-star feedbacks, it's time to start selling.

What should you sell?

Deciding what to sell is one of the most challenging decisions for most new sellers. But it doesn't have to be.

Chances are you have great things all around you—things that have been collecting dust for a long time on the shelves in your attic, garage, or basement.

Take a few minutes to walk around your house and gather up five or ten items to sell.

It's a great way to de-clutter and get rid of the stuff you've meant to throw out or sell at a yard sale over the years.

Do you have an old VCR that you never use anymore? Bundle it up with a stack of movies, and it could be a great seller. Many people swear by VCRs, especially the old ones, because the newer ones don't have tuners. Be sure to tell people if your VCR has a tuner. You could get more money from it.

I have a junk drawer with five or six old cell phones. Some of them work, and some of them don't. I bet I could bundle them up for a quick sale on eBay. What about your DVD collection? Have you stopped watching DVDs because it's more convenient to watch movies on demand from your cable and satellite provider or Netflix? Bundle them up, and you will score some quick cash on eBay.

Old video games are another quick seller on eBay. If your kids are anything like mine, they've gone through five or six video game systems over the last several years. Unfortunately, the old ones are stacked in the corners of their room or your living room. Sell those old game consoles on eBay and clear up some space.

Is your closet full of clothes you no longer wear? How about the kids? Younger kids outgrow their clothes every six months or even sooner. As a result, there is a huge market on eBay for used clothing, especially name brands or designer brands for adults or kids.

Are you beginning to understand? You probably have a minimum of fifty to one hundred items sitting around the house that buyers on eBay would love to get their hands on.

This is your opportunity to jump in and test the waters to see if selling on eBay is right for you.

Different ways to sell on eBay

There are several ways you can sell your items on eBay. Over time you will want to add them all to your toolbox.

Auctions are what made eBay famous. This is where items are listed, starting as low as a penny. The final selling price is determined by what people are willing to pay. With a bit of luck and a great description, that penny starting price can turn into fifty, even one hundred dollars or more if you can catch a wave of bidders.

Fixed Price listings are similar to shopping at Wal-Mart or Target. Sellers list their items for sale. Then, if a buyer wants the item, they can purchase it at the offered price.

Classified listings are an entirely different animal and are used more by businesses than everyday sellers. An example here would be a realtor trying to sell a home or a business. Classified listings capture leads and get people to call or email you. With a standard listing such as an auction or fixed price listing, sellers cannot include contact information such as a personal email address or a phone number. A classified listing allows you to work around this.

Other types of businesses you see using classified listings are website designers and people selling specialty advertising, such as custom imprinted shirts and pens.

eBay has several options that allow sellers to turbocharge their fixed price and auction listings.

Buy-it-now is an option sellers can add to items they sell at auction. It allows sellers to add a price to purchase the item immediately rather than waiting for the auction to end.

eBay requires the buy-it-now price to be at least 30% more than the starting bid. So, if you start your item at $10.00, your buy-it-now price must be at least $13.00. My suggestion is 30% is not a big enough jump.

When I run auctions with a buy-it-now, I shoot for the moon. In most cases, if I start my item at $9.99, I set my buy-it-now price at $27.99, and in one out of ten auctions that close successfully, I get the $27.99. On the other hand, when I'm selling a book I have a really good feeling about, sometimes I'll go crazy and set my buy-it-now price at $99.99, $179.99, or $249.99.

The cool thing is I frequently sell my items for that outrageous number because I take the time to craft a great description that builds value for my book. I get that number even when other sellers offer the same book with a $10.00 or $20.00 buy-it-now price.

Don't let yourself get suckered into playing the price game. Always offering the lowest price. It's all in how you position your items.

Best Offer is an option sellers can add to their fixed-price listings. Best offer allows sellers to be flexible on their asking price when using fixed-price listings.

Here's how it works. The seller sets the price, then allows buyers to send an offer. Pricing can be tricky because the offers you get will be all over the board.

What I've found is you tend to get three types of offers:

- They lowball you at $5.00 or $10.00, no matter your asking price.
- They offer you half of your asking price.
- They ask for a few bucks off to cover the cost of shipping.

So how do you handle best offers?

I put listings on auto-pilot whenever possible. That way, eBay doesn't bother sending me a bunch of lowball offers. The way this works is when you select best offer, eBay lets you set two options: 1) to decline all prices below a specific number and 2) to accept all offers above a certain amount. Doing this means you only need to deal with the offers where you can make money.

Sometimes I'll just say, what the hell, and accept the offer even though it's slightly less than I expected. But I often try to deal with the person making the offer and see if I can get them to bump their price up a notch or two.

The way I do this is to send them a counteroffer, along with a short note. For example, "Sorry, the best I can do is $15.00 plus shipping. It really is a nice item in excellent condition." The buyer can accept my offer, decline it, or send back a counter offer.

You will end up closing the sale about fifty percent of the time you send a counter offer, so you need to decide whether to take the first offer or shoot for a better deal.

Another option is to set a **reserve price** when selling with the auction format. A reserve price is probably not a good option unless you sell a valuable item. Most people will think your item is overpriced. A better strategy is to set a starting price you can live with and wait to see what happens.

How much does it cost to sell on eBay?

Fees add up quickly when you sell on eBay. I've had several months where eBay's take of my earnings was over $2,000.

There are two types of eBay sellers: those with eBay stores and those without.

No eBay store
. Up to 250 free auction listings per month
. Auction listings .30
. Additional fixed-price listings .30
. Final value fees are 12.9% in most categories

Starter Store
. $7.95 a month
. 250 free fixed-price listings / 250 auction listings
. Additional fixed-price listings .30
. Final value fees are 12.9% in most categories

Basic Store
. $27.95 a month/$21.95 with a subscription
. 1,000 /10,000 free fixed-price listings
. 250 free auction listings
. Additional fixed-price listings .25
. Final value fees are 12.9% in most categories

Premium eBay store
. $74.95 a month/$59.95 with a subscription
. 10,000 / 50,000 free fixed-price listings
. 500 free auction listings
. Additional fixed-price listings .10
. Final value fees are 12.9% in most categories

Anchor eBay store
. $349.95 a month/$299.95 with a subscription
. 25,000 / 75,000 free fixed-price listings
. 1,000 free auction listings
. Additional fixed-price listings .05
. Final value fees are 12.9% in most categories

There are additional fees for listing upgrades, such as buy-it-now, reserve auctions, and picture packs.

How do you sell on eBay?

Selling on eBay is easy once you understand a few of the basics.

Making a sale on eBay comes down to four things:

1. Craft a great title.
2. Write a benefits-driven description of the item you are selling.
3. Include close-up pictures that showcase your items from every angle.
4. Get the price right.

Your title is the number one sales tool available to you on eBay. It's how people find what you are selling.

eBay gives you 80 characters to get your message out there, so you need to get it right. The best strategy is to pack your title with keywords that help people find your item.

Don't worry about how your title reads.

It doesn't have to make any sense. However, it must include all possible combinations someone may use to search for your item. This includes the brand name, model number, version, year made, color, accessories included, new/used, warranty, and misspellings, if there are any common ones.

Here are a few great titles for iPads currently listed on eBay:

- Apple iPad 3rd Generation 16 GB Wi-Fi + Unlocked (Verizon) 9.7" – Black
- Brand New Apple iPad 3rd Generation 64 GB White WI-Fi + 4G (AT & T) 9.7" White (MD371LL/A)
- Apple iPad 3rd Generation 16 GB Wi-Fi Cracked Screen works
- Apple iPad 3rd Generation 16 GB Wi-Fi MC705LL/A Fully Functional Cracked Screen

Description. Good descriptions tell buyers everything they need to know about the item.

Your description should let potential buyers know who made the item, the model number, color, size, and condition. Is it new? Is it new in the box with tags? Is it gently used but in like-new condition?

Put yourself in the buyer's shoes for a moment. What would you need to know if you wanted to buy your item? If you're unsure what details to include, look at what other sellers say about similar things. Then, make a few notes, and include some of the better information in your description.

Be upfront about condition-related issues. Is there a scratch? Is there a chip in the paint? Are there some light grass stains on the knees of those jeans?

Be your own worst critic on eBay? Point out all of the flaws in the items you're selling. Better people should learn about any problems with your item before buying it than after it arrives on their doorstep. The last thing you want is negative feedback or to have to pay return shipping because you didn't properly describe your item.

Here are a few great descriptions to give you an idea of what you should say:

"1954 was the first year Hank, featured in the Topps #128 Hank Aaron baseball card, played as an outfielder for the Milwaukee Braves. A smart photograph of Hank Aaron with his full name and autograph is featured on the front of this 1954 card. The back of this Hank Aaron baseball card also supplies you with all his vital information and other major league records. Due to his immense popularity, this Hank Aaron baseball card is nearing the top of the record books in baseball history. Fun and amazing, the Topps #128 also makes a perfect gift for the baseball fan."

"You are bidding on an original 1958 Topps Mickey Mantle card #150. Look at the quality of this card, NICE! It is 100% authentic and unaltered, guaranteed. This card

has absolutely no creases. The corners have nice form with tip touches. The centering is superb, has perfect clear imagery, deep rich colors, shiny original gloss, and is clean, and the card has awesome eye appeal. There are no pinholes, markings, paper loss, stains, or other damage. This is a beautiful card of one of the game's greatest players—definitely a keeper. The card shown is the one you will receive. Please check the images; the card's quality will speak for itself."

They're great descriptions. They tell a good story, and what sets them apart is that many of the sellers in the sports card category post only one or two pictures with no description.

These guys make more sales because they take the time to craft killer descriptions.

Pictures. Pictures sell items. Make no mistake about it. Very few people will buy your item if you don't include at least one image. Therefore, more pictures are always better.

Ask yourself this, would you shell out $400 for a used laptop if you couldn't see a picture of it first? Probably not.

Suppose I was selling a rare Hummel figurine, and my description said it was in mint condition except for a small chip at the bottom of one leg. What would you think if I only showed you one picture of the figurine? You'd probably have doubts about that chip, wouldn't you? I could have easily closed the deal by including several close-up photos of the chipped area. Several well-shot, close-up pictures would make it easy to determine whether the chip is a bid stopper.

Take a good look at every item you sell. Put yourself in the buyer's shoes. What parts of the object would you need to see to decide if you want to buy that item? For example, for a baseball card, you need to see the front and back of the card. If you're selling a laptop, you probably want to see a picture of it with the Windows logo displayed on the screen as proof that it works. You'd also like a photo showing any accessories included with the laptop. This includes cords, cases, manuals, discs, and other goodies.

If you sell clothes, look at how some more successful sellers do it. They model their clothes on male and female manikins. This gives potential buyers a better reference for what they're buying than just looking at a flat picture of a blouse or pair of jeans. They include close-up images of designs and any flaws they described.

Price. Price is important, but it's only one piece of the puzzle. If you take the time to write an amazing title, craft a description that sells, and include plenty of close-up pictures, you're entitled to ask for a premium price.

Too many sellers let themselves get caught up in playing the price game. They get stuck with the mentality people only shop for price.

Most buyers will pay a little more if you give them a reason.

Think about the last time you shopped at one of the big box stores for a big-screen TV. You probably went to the store because the ad featured a 55" TV for $249.00. The salesman likely asked you a few questions before showing you that one. On the way to it, he stopped at a 65" Smart TV to show you how easily it hooks up to the internet through your Wi-Fi connection. He might have mentioned how easy watching movies on Netflix and Hulu is. Did he hand one of your kids a pair of 3D glasses so they could get a good look at the dinosaur popping out of the picture?

What happened next?

Odds are you bought the $999 Smart TV or the more expensive 3D TV because it had all of those great features you hadn't even thought about.

eBay buyers aren't any different than shoppers at a big box store. They might have every intention of grabbing the least expensive book or pair of jeans when they start shopping, but if you give them a compelling reason to spend a little more, they will open up their wallets and let a little more cash spill out.

My point is: If you're happy getting the same price everyone else is getting, go ahead and use the same lame-ass description everyone else is using. If you want the big bucks, consider each of your listings a work of art. Craft a compelling description that makes people beg you to take their money.

eBay tips and tricks

Now, I'm going to share a few secrets to help you step your game up a bit, so you can save time and make more money selling on eBay.

Brand your eBay store. One of the best things about eBay is that sellers can brand themselves. This means you can display your business name and logo in your listings. In addition, you can create a custom listing template and storefront that projects the image you want your customers to see.

eBay stores level the playing field and make it easier for you to compete with the big guys. They let you look like a big business, even if you're a one-man shop working part-time from your kitchen table.

A custom storefront allows you to offer your customers a unique shopping experience.

eBay sellers can create custom pages to share information and product details with their customers. The problem is very few sellers use them.

That's a big mistake!

Custom pages can greatly improve your customer's shopping experience and your sales. Here are a few ideas based on how I've seen eBay sellers use their custom pages:

- Include a sizing chart for clothing that explains how customers should take measurements.
- Show the measurements for each size for men's, women's, and children's clothing.
- Explain how your items are packaged and shipped (this is especially important if you have an upcharge for shipping because of the extra care you take in packaging items).
- Tips on how to take care of the items you sell.
- If you sell custom items, like imprinted clothing, pens, or mugs, explain what information you need from customers to make the project happen.
- Tell your story. What drove you to get into this business? What makes your business special? Why should customers buy from you rather than one of your competitors?
- If you sell graded sports memorabilia, explain what grading is and the different grading services you use.

- If you sell collectibles, you can explain how you grade your products.
- Design custom landing pages for different groups of your products.

Everything you do in your eBay store should help brand your business and brand you as an expert. Doing this increases confidence in your business and helps ensure buyers become repeat customers.

Designing a custom store isn't cheap, but it can double or even triple your business in the first few months you have it.

Automate your shipping. eBay and PayPal have some useful shipping tools integrated into them, but once you start selling more items or selling on multiple platforms, you will want a more advanced tool.

Stamps.com is run by the United States Post Office and helps sellers mail their products more efficiently. Using Stamps.com, sellers can import buyer information from eBay, Amazon, Etsy, and other marketplaces and print shipping labels on their home computers.

The reason I use Stamps.com is they let me ship first-class international packages without going to the post office. If you use the tools available on eBay, PayPal, and Amazon, the only international shipping options are Priority International and Express International (both of which are far too pricey for the items I sell).

Endicia provides mailing services similar to Stamps.com. In addition, they allow sellers to add a logo to their labels to help promote their brand.

Accept returns. If you want to play with the big boys, you must act like them. No one likes returns, but everyone likes sales. Accepting returns will encourage more people to buy from you.

When I started ramping up my sales on eBay, I offered "a 100% Money Back Guarantee. No questions asked."

Over the last twenty-two years, I've had less than ten returns. Probably fifty people have requested to return something, but after I let them know it wasn't a problem and I'd be happy to take their item back, most of them decided they would rather keep it.

Try offering a return policy, and see how it affects your business. If it doesn't work out for you, you can always change your policies down the road.

Create Special Sales. *Mark Down Manager* is a tool available to eBay store owners. You can access it in the *Marketing Tools* section of *Selling Manager*. Use it to create special sales for your customers or sell slow-moving inventory.

Sellers can use *Mark Down Manager* to discount items by category, or they can go through and select individual items to put on sale. The number of items you can put on sale at any time is determined by the level of eBay store you have.

It's not a sure thing. Sometimes it works better than others, but it's worth a shot if you need to raise some extra cash fast.

Be open to new ideas. Customer wants and needs change over time. Your eBay business needs to change with them.

Keep tabs on your competition, and watch what they are doing.

Hang out where your customers do online and listen to what they say. Are their favorite websites featuring new products? Pay attention to the trends you see happening and cater to them. You don't have to jump on the bandwagon and go at it full blast but take a few baby steps now and again. Try selling some new items. Some of them will work out. Some won't. The important thing is that you will carry more products your customers want and are willing to spend their money on.

Don't be afraid to change directions. It might be time to change directions if you've given it your best shot and it's not working. Maybe you need to change how you're branding yourself or presenting your product. Perhaps you need to kiss the old product line goodbye and reinvent yourself with a new product line.

There's no shame in reinventing your business. It's estimated most people will reinvent their careers at least three times throughout their work life. So why should your eBay business be any different?

Time to list your first item on eBay

Now it's time for a quick walk-through about how to sell on eBay.

The easiest way to start a listing is to search for the item you want to sell. Then, underneath the gallery pictures at the top of the listing page, you will see – "Have one to sell. Sell now."

Click where it says, "Sell it now." This brings up the sell your item form. It will walk you through the process, and you will have your item listed in no time.

Category. This is the category your item is listed in on eBay. Make sure it's the correct category for what you are selling. Research shows that 80% of sellers search by the item name, but 20% browse categories to discover new items when shopping. If you're in the wrong category, you could miss the opportunity to sell to these people.

Title. You get 80 characters to describe your item. Be sure you create a keyword-rich title loaded with terms buyers will use to search for your item.

Subtitle is an optional feature and costs from .50 to $1.50, depending on your listing style. Using a subtitle may be a good choice if you're listing a unique or a high-dollar value item. Remember that people can't search by the terms you include in your subtitle. Its primary purpose is to give buyers extra information so they can decide whether to click on your listing.

Subtitle costs extra, so only use it when you think it can help sell your item. Another thing to remember when you use subtitles, or other listing enhancers, is if your item doesn't sell, you'll pay that extra fee again and again when you relist it.

Keep track of when you use listing enhancers and remove them before you relist your item if you no longer want to use them.

Condition description lets you make a quick comment about any condition-related issues with your item. I like that it shows up right at the top of your listing. When you add comments here, tell people all of your item's faults, but be sure to word it, so that you minimize them.

If you sell rare books, you could word it like this, "This book has a few small pencil marks scattered throughout the first three chapters, but none of them interfere with reading the text. Other than this, the book is in very nice condition." Notice what I did. I told potential buyers the book had some defects (pencil marks), but otherwise, it was very nice. When you word your description this way, it creates the perception that the problem you listed isn't that bad.

Item Specifics change based on the item you are selling. You're not required to fill these out, but they can help you come up higher in search when people filter their search by size, color, etc. Also, some categories require item specifics, so check what you're selling.

Pictures. eBay gives you up to twelve free images with each listing. All photos are required to be:

- At least 500 pixels on the longest edge. eBay recommends 1600 pixels for the best picture quality when images are enlarged.
- Borders are not allowed around pictures.
- Sellers cannot add any text or artwork to their photos.
- At least one picture must be uploaded for every listing, even if you sell using eBay's catalog.

Gallery plus is a listing enhancement available for pictures. It's free for some categories. For others, there is a charge.

Description. Your item description can be entered in plain text or HTML. HTML is commonly used if you have an auction listing template or are trying to enhance the listing somehow.

If you use a template, you should paste it into this box and make whatever changes you need to customize it for this particular listing.

Themes. Themes are a form of a template. eBay charges ten cents for each listing you use them in. So my advice is to pass on themes. If you want to use a template to spruce up your listings, sign up for a service like Auctiva or Ink Frog. They host your pictures and include a wide selection of free templates.

Choose how you'd like to sell your item. Do you want to sell your item by auction or fixed price?

Both methods have their place. When it first started, eBay's main focus was on auctions. However, most of the action has shifted to fixed-price listings with no bidding over the last five years. Instead, people just click on the item and purchase it.

Everyone has a preference for which listing format is better. Much of it comes down to what you sell.

Suppose you list unique items where the selling price is unknown or frequently fluctuates, such as hot concert tickets or collectibles. In that case, the auction format should bring you a better price.

For commodity items or items that typically sell in a close price range, fixed-priced listings are generally a better choice.

If you have an item selling well, you may want to vary the length of your listings. For example, try one-day, three-day, five-day, seven-day, and thirty-day listings. Also, include buy-it-now on all of your auction listings, and use a higher price for your fixed-price listings. This strategy will maximize your sales and the final selling prices you receive for them.

If you sell in the auction format, enter your starting price—if you want to include a buy-it-now price, list it in the appropriate box. Below that, enter how many items you have to sell. Then, in the radio box for duration, select how long you want the listing to run.

Schedule start time allows you to decide when your item should start selling. eBay charges an extra ten cents to use this feature. My thought is there are plenty of buyers out there for your article whenever you decide to start and end it. Some people swear between 5:00 and 8:00 pm is the best time to end your listings. Other people insist Sunday is the best day. It's your dime—pick a strategy you like and run with it.

eBay Giving Works lets you sell your item for charity. You can donate anywhere from 10% to 100% of the selling price to your favorite charity when you sell with Giving Works. In addition, eBay will credit you back a portion of the selling fees when your item sells.

The nice thing about selling with eBay Giving Works is that thousands of local charities are signed up. So chances are you can easily discover ten or twenty local charities to support in your neck of the woods.

Charity listings draw more page views. In my experience, I often receive two to three times as many page views when I sell for a cause.

Getting Paid. eBay has transitioned to its managed payments system over the past year. For sellers used to Paypal, it's quite a change. All payments are made through eBay's payment system. eBay deducts fees as they are incurred. It takes one to two days to process the payment, and then they transfer funds to your bank account.

Shipping details. There are two sections you need to work with here. One is for domestic shipping (in your country), and the other is for international shipping (to foreign countries).

You have four shipping methods to choose from:

Flat rate shipping means you charge the same shipping rate to everyone regardless of where they are located. If you have a small item, such as a postcard or a book, you can tell everyone you will ship it for a certain amount. Sometimes it will cost you a little more, sometimes a little less. The good thing is flat rate shipping is easy to understand. If you say $4.00, everyone pays $4.00 for shipping.

Calculated shipping means you input the weight of your item into the shipping details, and eBay automatically calculates what shipping will be to the buyer's location. The shipping fees your buyer pays depend upon how much it costs to ship the item to them. When eBay displays the shipping amount, they figure it based on what it would be for that particular buyer. This is beneficial if you live closer to a buyer because your shipping could be less expensive than that offered by sellers who live further away.

Freight is calculated for shipments over 150 pounds. Freight shipping is for larger and heavier items that need to ship by an over-the-road truck line.

Local pickup means the buyer can pick the purchase up at the seller's location. Sellers select this option when the item they're selling is fragile or bulky and hard to pack. I've seen buyers use it with furniture, exercise equipment, or when they are selling a large collection of books. Because the items are large and difficult to pack, the sellers often don't want to go to the trouble and expense of doing it, so they limit shipping to local pickup only.

International shipping. Many sellers are afraid to offer international shipping because they're unsure how it works. The truth is shipping internationally is no more complicated than shipping in your own country. The major difference is you need to include a custom tag with most international shipments that lists the contents of the package and its value.

Your local post office can walk you through it the first few times, or if you are printing shipping labels online, the programs will walk you through all the steps.

I would suggest setting delivery expectations for your customers. When you mail the package, send a quick email to your customer telling them their shipment is on the way. You may want to say something like this in the email, "Thank you for your order. It was mailed today. Normal international delivery time is two to three weeks, but can take as many as six to eight weeks depending upon customs and local post offices." Doing this will save you a lot of customer service emails from customers who don't receive their packages the following week.

eBay also has something called the Global Shipping Program. It makes shipping items internationally as easy as mailing them within your home country. Select the Global Shipping Program under the international shipping options when listing your item to opt into the program. When an item sells internationally, eBay notifies you to send it to one of its shipping partners within the United States. When the package reaches the shipping center, your responsibility for it is done. The shipping center repackages the item, fills out customs forms, and sends it. (eBay changed its Global Shipping Program in the fall of 2022, but buyers and sellers will notice very few differences.)

Other things you'd like buyers to know. The first item here allows you to set bidder requirements, such as not allowing bidders with two or more recent non-paying bidder strikes to bid on your auctions.

If you have a sales tax permit, select the state where you want to collect sales tax and the amount to collect. Then, if your item sells in that state, eBay will collect tax on the item for you and list it separately on the invoice for you and your buyer.

In most cases, you don't need a sales tax permit to sell on eBay. They automatically collect the taxes in states that require it.

Return policy. At this time, eBay does not require you to accept returns, but I would strongly recommend doing so. It will increase your sales. If you decide to accept returns, check the boxes by how long the buyer has to return the item and who pays return shipping – the buyer or the seller. You should also state a return policy in the box provided. Mine is, *"Here at history-bytes, we understand that buying items sight unseen on the internet can sometimes be scary. For this reason, we offer a 100 % MONEY-BACK GUARANTEE. You can return your item within 30 days for a full refund – No Questions Asked."*

The final box on this page allows you to list any additional checkout instructions.

The bottom of the page will show you **your fees so far**—after this click, continue to move on to the next page.

At the top of the next page, eBay takes one more shot at selling you some of their listing enhancements, such as gallery plus, subtitle, and bold. But, again, my advice is to just say no! Unless you have something special, selecting any options will be like throwing your money down the garbage disposal.

At the bottom of this page, it once again reviews your fees. If everything looks good, click on list your item, and it will go live on eBay. If you want to see how it looks, click on preview listing, which will generate a preview of your listing for you to review.

....

Selling on eBay can be easy, fun, and profitable.

My advice is to baby-step it. Try listing a few items you have around the house. Then, if you decide eBay is a good opportunity for you, start looking for a niche you can fill and begin targeting products to it.

Build your business slowly. Keep testing new products, discarding the losers, and keeping the winners. Over time you will discover you have a strong business with a steady stream of repeat buyers.

Sell it on Amazon

The best thing about Amazon is the low cost of entry.

Unlike eBay and many other online commerce sites, Amazon doesn't have separate listing fees for the items you put up for sale. As a result, sellers can add thousands of items to their Amazon store without paying fees until they sell something.

Another great thing about selling on Amazon is you can list most of your items in one minute or less. You don't have to snap any pictures. You don't have to write a detailed item description. Selling your item on Amazon is as simple as hitching a ride on the Amazon listing page.

It's easy to spot the items listed by individual sellers. When you see a box like the one below, the items sold by Amazon are listed under Amazon's price. The items offered by individual sellers are in the following two categories.

Formats	Amazon price	New from	Used from
Kindle Edition	$3.77	--	--
Paperback	$10.54 ✓Prime	$10.54	$14.39

What I want to do first is take a minute to walk you through listing a typical item for sale on Amazon. Then I will give you some pointers about maximizing your sales there.

Listing your first item on Amazon

Type the name or the description of the item you want to sell into the Amazon search bar. Click on the thing you want to sell. Off to the right-hand side, you will see a small box labeled **more buying choices**. At the bottom of this box, click on the **Sell on Amazon** button.

At this point, you're eight steps away from listing your item for sale on Amazon.

Step 1. Amazon shows you the title and picture of the item you selected and asks you to verify this is the correct item you want to sell. You don't need to do anything if it's the right item.

Step 2. Tell customers your item's condition. Click on the radio button in the box labeled **condition** and select the one that best describes the condition of your item.

Below this, you have a chance to add a comment about the condition of your item. For example, suppose you are selling a textbook. In that case, you could say, "overall, excellent condition, but it does have some highlighting in the first three chapters."

Step 3. Amazon shows you the lowest price the item is being sold for and the lowest shipping price available for it. In most cases, you will find that Amazon has the lowest price, especially if you sell new items and offer free shipping (with Amazon prime). Don't panic! Many people will still buy from you, even if your price is higher and you charge shipping.

Step 4. Enter your selling price. Next to the box where you enter your selling price, Amazon shows how much they will charge your customer for shipping.

Step 5. Tell Amazon how many items you have for sale.

Step 6. This step tells Amazon to collect taxes if you have enabled them to do so. Casual sellers can skip this step. Instead, Amazon collects taxes in the states that require it.

Step 7. Enter your SKU (stock-keeping unit). This is how you identify the item you are listing for sale. I have over

10,000 items available for sale on Amazon. All of them are numbered and stored on storage shelves. I can go to that shelf whenever one sells and quickly pull the item for shipping.

When you are just starting a SKU isn't all that important, but if you intend to grow your business, you should start thinking about using some type of labeling system.

Amazon assigns one for you if you decide not to enter a SKU.

Step 8. Select your shipping methods. Amazon requires you to add a basic shipping service. Adding additional shipping options can help you sell more items. I suggest choosing Expedited Shipping (priority mail) and the first international shipping option (first class).

At this point, you're almost done. Press the yellow **Continue** button at the bottom.

This takes you to a screen to review your selling information. The last few boxes show you Amazon's commission when your item sells, how much Amazon allows you for shipping, and how much money you will receive (including your shipping credit) after Amazon's commission is taken out.

If everything looks good, press the **Submit your listing** button.

The next thing you're going to see is
Congratulations! You've successfully listed _____.

That's it. Your item is now listed for sale on Amazon.

You can sit back and wait for the sales to start rolling in, or better yet, list more items so you can make more sales.

For most items you sell, that is all there is to selling on Amazon.

How to add an item to the Amazon catalog

Suppose you sell unique items that aren't already in the Amazon catalog. In that case, Amazon lets you add an item description page to their catalog. While it's not hard to do, it does take a little extra time and effort, so I will cover this in more detail.

To add an item to the Amazon catalog, you need to visit Seller Central and place your mouse over **Inventory**. Then, at the drop-down menu, select **Add a Product**.

Find it on Amazon

Enter your product name, UPC, EAN, ISBN or ASIN   [Search]

If it is not in Amazon's catalog: [Create a new product]

This allows you to search the Amazon catalog to see if it is already listed. Suppose your item is not currently available on Amazon. In that case, you can add a new item by clicking on **Create a new product**.

Select a category to list your item in. You can search for a category or browse through a list of categories. Choose the category that most closely fits your item.

After selecting the category you want to list your item in, you will be taken to the sell your item dashboard.

Provide as much information as possible under each of the six tabs at the top of your dashboard. Try to fill in every box you can because Amazon will use your information to show your item in relevant search requests.

At the very least, you need to fill in the boxes with a red star to the left of them.

Vital Info. What you put here is going to become the title for your listing. Make sure it is keyword-rich and describes your item correctly. You have 250 characters to state your case. Make the most of it. Give the name, manufacturer, model number, color, accessories, and other familiar names your item might be known by.

The manufacturer is exactly what it says. If you know who made your item, list it here. If you know the brand name, enter it in the following line. Next, enter the model number and manufacturer number if they are available. Package quantity means how many are packaged together – one, two, or a dozen. Finally, the UPC or EAN is the manufacturer's product code. If you know the UPC code, enter it here.

Offer. List your selling price—just below that, you can offer a sale price for a limited period. Enter the sale price, and select the days you would like the sale to run. Enter how many items you have. If you have a sales tax permit, enter the pertinent info so that Amazon can collect sales tax from your buyers.

Handling time means how many days it will be before shipping the item. Amazon's default is one or two days, so list it here if it takes longer to get your item ready to ship. An example of this would be if you use a drop shipper, and it takes some time for the order to process through their system.

The selling date is when you want the item listed on Amazon. Gift options: Will you gift wrap the item or include a card with it. Select the services you wish to offer. Restock date means if you are out of stock, when will more be available.

Import designations tell buyers where your item was made. Several choices are available. Read through them and choose the most appropriate one for what you are selling.

Next, you need to choose your shipping method. You can ship the item or offer fulfillment by Amazon (FBA). FBA means you shipped your products to Amazon when you listed them, and Amazon handles shipping and fulfillment for you. The biggest advantage is that your items often qualify for Amazon's free shipping offers, including Amazon Prime. Another advantage is many buyers are more comfortable buying from you because your item ships to them directly from Amazon.

I will talk about Fulfillment by Amazon and how it can help to increase your sales in more detail later in this chapter.

Images. You need to include at least one photo of your item. The more pictures you include, the better your chances of selling your item. Picture requirements are listed next to the uploading tool.

When getting pictures ready to upload, you should keep in mind the following:

- Only show the exact item you are selling. Do not include any extra items or props in your pictures.
- Watermarks are not allowed.
- You cannot superimpose any text over your images.
- Your main image must be a photo. Drawings are not allowed.
- All pictures should be a minimum of 1000 x 500 pixels. Buyers cannot zoom in on smaller images, so they will not have close-up views of what you are selling.
- J-Peg illustrations are the preferred file type.

Description. The description section is broken down into two sections. One is for product features, and the next section is for your actual written description of the item.

Features give more information about your item and are listed in bullet points on the item description page. Here are some of the features provided for the Apple iPad to give you an idea of what type of features you should list with your items:

- Apple's newest generation of iPads
- 9.7 inch (diagonal) LED glossy back-lit screen
- Forward-facing and rear camera

- Apple IOS 4 and access to the Apple Apps store
- 1 GHz dual-core Apple A5 custom-designed processor

Your description should be written in a narrative style and product-focused. You are not allowed to include any information about your business.

Once you list your item, the item description page becomes part of the Amazon catalog. Therefore, any seller with the same item can list it alongside yours on the same item description page.

Keywords. Keywords are similar to tags you put on your items to help buyers find them in search. You can skip the first section of keywords as it is only available to Platinum Sellers.

Search terms are the keywords buyers will use to search for your items. Include all obvious ones: Product name, model #, manufacturer, color, and size. If you have trouble thinking of keywords, visit the Google Keyword Tool. It will help you pick keywords people use to search for your item.

Another word of advice—don't use single-word search terms. Instead, use "long-tail keywords" whenever possible. Long-tail keywords are more specific and encompass most of the searches made on Google. Some examples of long-tail keywords are: "Space exploration in the Milky Way Galaxy," "How to write better keywords," and "How to make money on Kindle."

The following section helps Amazon determine how your product is used and on what occasions it is used. This allows Amazon to show your items in a variety of searches.

More Details. This section lets you add more product-specific information. Some categories include Brand, MSRP, Part number, model number, and is your item subject to prop. 65 reporting in California, shipping weight, product and shipping size specifications, and the like. Specific information is based on the type of product you are selling.

When you are done, press **Save and finish**. Your item is now listed for sale on Amazon.

It sounds complicated, but it will be a lot easier after you've added two or three products to the catalog.

The biggest problem when I add custom pages is that there's no real-time preview like you have on eBay. It can take a half-hour or more for the listing page to display on Amazon, so you have to check back later to ensure everything posted okay. Another problem is that pictures can take ten or fifteen minutes to upload, so you're stuck waiting before you can work on your next product listing.

That pretty much covers listing your items on Amazon.

If you have a large catalog of items, you can upload them through a spreadsheet. In addition, several services help eBay sellers move their entire eBay store to Amazon.

One such service I have had experience with is Export Your Store.

I like using Export Your Store because they do all the heavy lifting for you. The bad thing about using Export Your Store is that Amazon is nothing like eBay, so after they transfer your items to Amazon, you still have a lot of work to ensure everything is properly optimized.

Here are a few differences between eBay and Amazon that can cause problems.

- Amazon is a marketplace. Therefore, they don't allow personal branding or HTML code on item description pages.
- Amazon doesn't allow references to your business in their item description pages.
- Amazon requires tags (keywords) to be entered in the proper section of their listing form to help buyers find your item in a search.

The folks at Export Your Store are really good at stripping the HTML code out of your listings and getting them moved over to eBay. I had over ten thousand items exported from eBay to Amazon in just over two days.

Then I started receiving a stream of item violation warnings from Amazon. When I did this, you could still have your customer service email address in your eBay listings. This violated Amazon's terms of service, and I was forced to go through just over 10,000 items, one at a time, and edit each of them individually.

Three weeks of hell followed, spending twelve to fourteen hours daily checking, revising, and deleting listings.

Another problem was that when they stripped the HTML code from my listing templates, they removed part of my item descriptions, including the SKU numbers. As a result, I had to add keywords to every Amazon listing. I think this was because I sell one-of-a-kind collectibles, and each item required adding a new page to the Amazon catalog. Of course, this would not be an issue if you sell more traditional items, like electronics, books, CDs, or DVDs that already have a catalog page.

I would still recommend Export Your Store with all the problems I mentioned. Customer service was responsive and worked quickly to help solve any issues.

Several other companies can help you export your eBay store items to Amazon. Two of them are Vendio and Linnworks.

Amazon FBA

Amazon FBA (Fulfillment by Amazon) can help skyrocket your sales. According to a study conducted by Amazon, 64% of people who have used Fulfillment by Amazon have increased their sales by 20% or more.

When you use Fulfillment by Amazon, Amazon becomes customer service central for your business.

Here are the top benefits you receive by using FBA:

1. Your items become eligible for FREE Super Saver Shipping and Amazon Prime Benefits
2. Your FBA items are displayed with no shipping charges, giving you the benefit of being a lower-priced seller
3. Your back end is taken care of by Amazon. They handle all of the shipping, returns, and customer service problems for you.
4. Your items become eligible to compete for the Buy Box.

Using FBA frees up more time to source new products and enjoy life more.

You ship your inventory to Amazon's warehouse. Once they receive your items in their inventory, they go for sale on Amazon. Each time one of your items sells, you will see it show up in your seller dashboard, but the good folks at Amazon do all of the work for you. They collect your payment. They ship the order for you and handle all customer service issues or returns.

Compare that with being an eBay Top Rated Seller who must ship their item with a one-day handling time to receive their 20% final discount fee. eBay sellers are chained to their computers, while Amazon FBA sellers are free to enjoy life without the constant rush to ship and handle customer service issues.

FBA is also a great deal for Amazon buyers.

FBA assures customers they will receive a great experience when buying from you. Most of the items sold through FBA are eligible for Amazon Super Saver Shipping and other Amazon Prime Benefits, including free shipping on orders over $25.00.

How to get started with FBA

To get started using FBA:

1. List your items in seller central, and select Fulfillment by Amazon as your shipping choice.
2. If you already have the item for sale on Amazon, go to **Manage Your Inventory** on your Seller Central Dashboard. Then, select the product that you want to include as FBA.

3. Print the labels provided by Amazon to ship your items to their warehouse.
4. When Amazon receives and scans your items into its inventory, they go live and are ready for sale.

Sell it on Etsy

Etsy is a community of crafters who buy and sell handmade items. Sellers can also offer crafting supplies and certain vintage items.

A visit to the Etsy home page reveals several subtle differences between eBay and Amazon. First, Etsy has all the normal product pictures towards the top of the home page. Then, as you scroll further down the page, you find a link to one of Etsy's featured sellers, along with several pictures of products he has for sale.

Today's featured seller is Jeff Libby, better known on Etsy as birdloft. After you click the link, you are taken to a photo interview loaded with pictures of Jeff making some of his custom wood birdhouses. Below this interview, you can visit recently featured sellers like Sarah with Blue Birds Fly Boutique.

You will find several recent posts to the Etsy blog below the featured seller listings. Next to that are "The Top Ten Marketing Tips from Full Time Etsy Sellers."

Today's tips are from Amy, and her first recommendation is a good one "Make your pictures drool-worthy!"

It's a folksy downhome feeling, and it permeates the entire site. It's friendly, inviting, and buyer and seller oriented – Something eBay used to be back in the day before they started kissing up to the big sellers.

You need to know that Etsy is focused on helping artists, crafters, woodworkers, and other makers of handmade items sell their wares. Sellers can also offer crafting supplies and some vintage items as long as they are over twenty years old.

Getting started

Look for the big red button that says Etsy in the upper left-hand corner to get started. Then, click the gray button next to it that says **register** and fill in the required information.

As with all e-commerce sites, your user name is the most critical decision to make when registering.

I encourage you to take some time to think it through. Your name should tell people a little bit about your business and the type of products you sell. Of course, many people on Etsy choose to use their name, which is fine. But, on Etsy, your brand is all about you and the products you make.

After you signup up, you should begin to fill in your profile so buyers can get to know you better. You will see a link in the upper right corner that says **Hi username**. Click on that. It will bring you to Etsy's profile page. Click where it says **edit profile**.

The first thing you should do is add a profile picture. I suggest a photo of you surrounded by some of your crafts or working on a project. If you're feeling a little shy and don't want to include yourself in the picture, pick one of your favorite projects and upload an image.

Continue filling out this form. Add as much information as you can. For example, if you want to change your user name, you can change it here. The last few lines at the bottom of this section let you select where you would like to share your profile information. By default, Etsy checks all of these so your profile information will appear in as many places as possible. Uncheck any information you would rather not share.

Over to the right-hand side of the screen, you will see your control panel. Click on Settings, and continue adding information to your profile.

Account. If you have a Facebook or Twitter account, you can link them to your Etsy account here. You can also update your email address and password or close your account.

Preferences allow you to set contact information and other such info from Etsy. Use this area to select your location and currency preference. At the top, you can filter out mature (XXX) items so they are not shown in your search results. Etsy has them filtered out by default, so you must turn them on if you wish to receive mature selections.

Privacy allows you to select who can see your favorites and whether people can search for you by email address.

Security gives you additional methods to help secure your account online. However, they are switched off by default, and you must manually turn them on.

Shipping address is just what it says. Enter your full mailing address here.

Credit cards lets you put a credit card on file with Etsy.

Emails allows you to select your email settings and what emails you would like to receive from Etsy and your customers.

Make sure you bookmark this page. It's loaded with useful tools you can integrate into your Etsy business.

If you have a website, a cool tool named Etsy Mini lets you build a widget to sell your Etsy items on your website.

Fees

Etsy's fees are inexpensive and easy to understand. First, there is a listing fee of .20 for each item, which runs for four months. Then, there is a 5% final value fee when your item sells.

Fees are accrued for the month, and you are emailed a billing statement at the end of the month. All payments are due by the 15th of the month.

Etsy Shop

All sellers can open an Etsy Shop. Your shop is your spot on Etsy, where you can brand yourself and your business. Etsy has a guide to help you get started.

You should also visit the seller handbook.

The manual does a good job walking you through setting up and customizing your Etsy Shop.

Follow these steps to set up your shop:

Give your shop a name. Remember what we said earlier. Make it unique, and make sure it describes your business. Barring that, use your name.

Upload a banner to customize your shop further. Picture requirements are 760 x 100 pixels. If you're unsure where to get a banner, head over to Fiverr. They have a lot of designers that will make you a fantastic banner starting at $5.00.

Add a shop announcement. According to the Etsy blog, the first 160 characters of your shop announcement appear in search when people search for your item using Google, Yahoo, and Bing. So make it short, descriptive, and compelling to entice searchers to click into your shop.

Add shop sections. This section is similar to categories in an eBay store. You are allowed ten sections to separately call out different product lines, items, or sizes.

Add shop policies. This is where you share information with your customers about how you do business. The main thing to remember is to keep your messages customer-friendly. Too many sellers use strings of negative words like "I don't," "I won't, "Checks and money orders will not be accepted."

It's ok to say what you will and won't do, but find a nice way of saying it. People don't like being told what they can't do. Instead, they want to hear, "this is what we can do for you."

You can include specific policies: Welcome Message, Payment Policy, Shipping Policy, Refund Policy, Additional Information, and Seller Information.

Set up how to get paid

There are several tabs at the top of your shop page. To set up your payment methods, click on the **Get Paid** tab.

The first option you see is Direct Checkout. This option lets buyers pay for items through Etsy using credit or debit cards. You are charged 25 cents per order plus 3% of the order total for using this service.

If you're a new seller, Etsy makes your funds available within three days or as soon as you ship the item, whichever comes first. After selling for 90 days, funds are made available to you the next business day.

You can add additional payment methods by checking the link under the direct checkout box.

Listing your first item

Now that your shop is set up, it's time to list your first item.

Who made it? Choices are: I did, a member of my shop, or another company or person. Select the one that applies.

Categories. Use the drop-down menu, and select the category that best describes your item.

Add variations. Variations are differences in your product listings, such as size, color, etc. When buyers select your item, they must choose the variations they want.

Keep in mind that variations don't show up in searches. So if you want the size, color, etc., to be searchable, you should set up a separate listing.

Photos. You can add up to five pictures to your listing. Make sure they are clear photos showing all the details of what you are selling. If you have fancy frill work or designs, include a few close-ups.

Invest in a lightbox so you can take well-lit close-up photos. You can find them for $30 to $40 on eBay and Amazon. What a lightbox does is help to diffuse the light so you can take a good clear picture of your item. In addition, most lightboxes come with several backdrops in various colors to bring out the contrast in your photographs.

Title. The key to writing a good title is to understand your title is the search string for your listing. It is how people find your listing on Etsy.

Think about every feature your item has. What terms will buyers use to search for your item? What names or terms is it known by? What period is it from? The renaissance, 70's, 90's punk? Then, pick out the most important terms you can think of and pack them into the title.

Description. This is where you do your selling. Tell people what your item is and how it was made? What makes your item special compared to everybody else's?

Give people a compelling reason to buy your item. Tell them what's in it for them. For example, if it is hand-stitched, tell people. Let people know how you made it or what materials you used.

The more detailed information you include, the better your chances of selling it.

Shop section. If you set up shop sections, which section do you want to include it in.

Recipient. Who is this item for? Most times, you will want to leave this one blank. You don't want to limit your chances of selling it by targeting just one type of buyer.

Occasion. Will it be used for a special event? Again, like recipient, leave this one blank unless you are sure it is for only one occasion, such as a wedding or a prom.

Style. Choose two styles that describe your item from the drop-down list.

Tags. Like your title, you want to load your tag section with keywords people will use to search for your item. Obvious keywords are style, color, size, use, etc. Use as many phrases as possible that describe your item or what it is used for – prom dress, wedding dress, linen tablecloth, or custom-made lace and satin prom dress.

Put yourself in your buyer's shoes for a minute. What words would you use to search for your item? Etsy gives you thirteen tags. Use every one of them.

Materials. You can choose up to thirteen materials your item is made with.

Price. Enter your price here.

Quantity. How many of these items do you have for sale?

Shipping. The first thing you are asked for is the processing time. How soon will you ship your item? Next, choose the country your item is shipping from.

In the ships to section, you can set your pricing. Set your price for domestic shipping first.

If you plan on shipping internationally, the first box will let you ship anywhere and set a price. If you only want to ship to certain countries, you can choose them from the drop-down box and price shipping to each country individually.

When you set a shipping price, include the cost of boxes, envelopes, bubble wrap, labels, tape, and driving to and from the post office. You don't want to set your price so high as to discourage people from buying from you, but you should try to cover your costs.

Another option is to offer free shipping and roll the shipping cost into the price of your item.

Whatever you do, keep your shipping costs competitive with other sellers offering similar items.

Preview your item. If everything looks good, press enter to send your listing live.

That's it. You've listed your first item on Etsy. Once you have four or five listings under your belt, it will get quicker.

....

You now know how to set up your Etsy shop, list your items for sale, and how to discover items to sell and at what prices they are currently selling.

Get started today, and keep experimenting with new products and tweaking your Etsy shop. Success will follow your hard work.

Check out these books

- Etsy-preneurship: Everything You Need to Turn Your Handmade Hobby into a Thriving Business by Jason Malinak.
- Etsy Selling Success: Cash in on Your Creations by Elyse Reynolds.
- Starting an Etsy Business for Dummies by Allison Strine and Kate Shoup.
- Etsy Success Stories: Conversations with Etsy's Top Sellers by Vivian Atenujmobi.
- How to Price Crafts and Things You Make to Sell by James Dillehay.
- Etsy 101: Sell Your Crafts Online, the DIY Marketplace for Handmade, Vintage, and Crafting Supplies by Steve Weber.

Kindle Book Marketing

I've been publishing books on Kindle for nearly twelve years now, and it really is one of the best ways to make money online.

It's also a lot of work.

Many "Gurus" out there market books and courses, saying Kindle books are a good source of passive income. Trust me. They're anything but passive. If you expect to keep the money rolling in, you need to be constantly tinkering with this and tweaking that. But, more on all of that later.

One book normally isn't going to make you a lot of money. The real magic starts as you grow your backlist and have eight to ten books in print.

So how do you get started?

- You need a great idea.
- You need to produce a well-written book.
- You need to publish your book.
- Just because you published a book doesn't mean anybody will buy it. You need to get the word out to help people find your book.
- The Kindle world has very few one-book wonders. So, if you want to make money writing, the best

advice I can give you is as soon as you're done writing a book, get started writing your next book.

Successful book ideas

Finding a book topic is a lot like shopping for a new car. You really have to work at it to find the right one. I need to try it on and make sure it's going to be a good fit for me. After all, I'm going to spend several months working on it. If I don't like the topic, chances are no one else will either.

Normally I start by brainstorming topics. I put together a list of twenty or thirty possible topics and then narrow it down. When I've got my list down to three or four ideas, I explore them in more detail.

The first thing I do is type my idea into the Amazon search bar to get a quick overview of what's out there. I want to know how many books have been written on my topic, how well they sell, and how different authors approach the subject.

The nice thing about doing your initial research on Amazon is you get to explore current books that are selling now. When you find one that sounds interesting, look at the description. If it has possibilities take a peek inside. Amazon lets you read the first ten percent of most books so that you can check out the table of contents, the writing style, and some of the information offered inside.

Don't stop there. Check out some of the reviews. Most of them will only be a line or two. They normally won't tell you much, maybe whether the writer liked the book or not. Some of the longer reviews detail what they liked or hated about it. The really good reviews tell you what they wished would have been included in the book.

This is all gold. Use it to help shape your book into something readers want. Make sure you have your notebook handy and take copious notes during your research.

Another great piece of information you can pick up on Amazon is how well books on your topic sell. Midway down the book description page is a section titled "Product Details." It shows the book's "Amazon Best Seller Ranking." If the book is ranked in a category, it will show you its ranking and categories.

The lower the number, the better the book is selling. Most authors look for several books in a category to be ranked at 20,000 or lower. This means the book sells four to six copies daily, which gives you a shot at making some decent money. A ranking of 50,000 means the book sells one to two copies a day, and a ranking of 100,000 means the book sells one or two copies a week. A ranking above 500,000 means the book is selling one copy a month.

Unless you've got a great message or some startling discovery, you probably want to table an idea if there aren't at least one or two books in the category that rank under 20,000.

Produce a Well-Written Book

You don't have to be another Stephen King or Amanda Hocking, but you need to know how to turn a phrase.

If you write nonfiction, readers will be more forgiving of grammatical errors as long as you deliver the information you promised. However, if you're writing a novel, people expect to be entertained, and you had better be at the top of your game if you want to make big sales.

No book is ever perfect, especially on the first go around. Therefore, every book should go through several rounds of proofreading for grammatical errors and typos.

One of the fastest ways to get your book torn apart in the Kindle market is to publish a poorly written book loaded with typos. It's going to put you on the fast track to bad reviews. So, it will not only tank this book but probably your next one, too.

If you're not up to editing your book, ask a friend who is good with English. Another option is to hire a proofreader or copy editor on Fiverr or another freelancing site.

Get Your Manuscript Ready For Publication

It's relatively easy to publish your book on Kindle.

I've read a lot of complicated descriptions describing how to properly format your manuscript in HTML or with this or that eBook program. The truth is – you can do it just as well in MS Word.

Here are a few tips for taming your manuscript with Word.

- Set your page margins to six inches times nine inches.
- Don't paste your pictures into the text. Instead, use Word's insert picture function. This ensures your pictures are displayed properly.
- Insert a page break after each section. This will give your readers a better reading experience by starting each new section on a fresh page.
- Stick with the basic fonts. Use Arial, Calibri, or Times Roman in either 11 or 12-point size type.
- Don't format your eBook like you would a print book. People will read your eBook on different reading devices – Kindle, PC, Phone, and Tablets. Readers can change the font and typestyle for

most books. Everything else will be fine if your basic layout is good.
- Add a clickable table of contents to your book. This is easier than it sounds and will make your book appear more professional.

To get started: Go through your manuscript and highlight the chapter titles. After highlighting each chapter title, click on *Heading 1* in the *Home* section of the toolbar. Do this for each chapter.

Next, highlight all of your sub-headings, and select Heading style 2. This will differentiate them from the chapter titles when they appear in your table of contents.

The last step is to add your table of contents. Go to a blank page where you want to insert your table of contents. Click on the *References* tab in the upper toolbar. At the far left, you will see *Table of Contents*. Click on it. Select *Insert Table of Contents*. A little further down, you will see a checkmark saying *Show Page Numbers*. Click on the box with the checkmark to remove it. Click OK at the bottom of the page.

One last step and you're done.

Type the words "Table of Contents" at the top of the page. Highlight it, and select *Insert Bookmark*. Type "toc," where it asks you to insert the *bookmark name*. This tells Kindle this is your table of contents and will make it available to readers as a menu option.

Publish Your Book

There are many options available to authors who want to self-publish their books. The more popular sites are Kindle, Barnes & Noble, Smash Words, Kobo, and iTunes.

I recommend starting with Kindle and branching out to other sites after you've got some sales under your belt.

I recommend Kindle because they currently control over 65 percent of the eBook market. You're a writer. You might as well go where the readers are, right?

Go to the Kindle sign-up screen, and follow the directions to sign up for a Kindle Direct Publishing account.

When you're ready to publish your book, select *Add a New Title*.

The first option you're offered is to *Enroll this book in KDP Select*. My suggestion is to check this box. KDP is an amazing way to promote your book on Amazon. Every ninety days, Amazon lets you give away free downloads of your book for five days. Two other options to help you sell books are Kindle Countdown Deals and Kindle Unlimited. We will talk more about them later in this chapter.

Book description

Your book description is how readers determine whether they want to buy your book.

Some authors write very short descriptions. That's a waste of valuable real estate. Your description needs to tell people what your book is about. It should be informative, enticing, and written in a style similar to your book. You don't want to give away the farm, but you want to give readers a reason to click the buy button.

I like to ask a question and then go into more detail. Sometimes authors begin with a shocking fact or startling statistic. Other writers start their descriptions by showing portions of the reviews they've received.

There's no right or wrong way to write your description. Make it fit you and your book. For example, if your book is short and very little appears in the preview, you may want to include an excerpt in your description.

Target your book

You enter two key details here.

The first thing you're asked to do is select two categories for your book. The category your book lands in can make or break your book.

There are millions of books for sale on Amazon. Readers find new books using one of two methods. Either they type keywords into the search bar or browse categories. Your book must be ranked among the top 100 in its category to be found by browsers. Unfortunately, many people only look at the top 20 books in a category before clicking away.

So the category you choose will play a big part in determining the success of your book.

Some authors suggest you pick easy categories starting out to ensure your book will rank high. Instead, they put their books in marginal categories that don't fit their title best. I've always gone for the category I want to rank in. If my book is a presidential biography, that's the category I choose. If my book is about selling on eBay, I prefer the e-commerce category in business and computers.

If you're in doubt, check what categories your closest competitors are listed in and go with those. Then, after your book has been on the site for a while, Amazon will slot your book into the categories they think it will sell best in.

Next, you need to select keywords people will use to search for your book.

The keywords you choose are crucial to the success of your book. For example, the keywords I chose for this book are Kindle publishing, self-publishing guide, eBay business, eBay guidebook, how to sell on Amazon, how to sell on Fiverr, and Kindle Unlimited.

None of my keywords are single words. Think about how you search for a book. You might start with eBay, then move out to eBay Profits or online auction sales. Some authors suggest you include the names of popular authors and book titles. The problem is doing that violates Amazon's terms of service and could get your book pulled from the site.

As the book starts to sell, I keep refining my list of keywords until I get down to seven I feel will get the job done.

Remember, you can change keywords anytime, so try changing your keywords if your book isn't selling. Give them at least a week to see what happens. If you don't see an increase in sales, keep tweaking your keywords until you're happy with the results.

Upload book cover and book file

Best advice you will ever get. Never design your book cover, no matter how good you think you are.

Here's a review of one of my books received with a self-designed cover: "Got this during a free promo. No way I would have paid money for it with this cheesy cover, but it's actually a decent book."

People say you can't judge a book by its cover, but everybody does.

Think about the last time you bought a book. One of two things caught your eye: The title or the cover. Maybe, a little bit of both.

A great cover doesn't need to be expensive. You can commission someone to create custom artwork and get the most unique design. However, that can easily cost you $500, $1000, or more. So, I take a slightly different approach and hire several designers on Fiverr to create a cover for me. This gives me several covers to choose from, and I can put the best one on Kindle.

This also gives me a fallback strategy. If sales aren't what I expect, I switch out my covers and see if it helps sales.

Note: Over the last two years, I've used 99 Designs to create most of my coves. It's more expensive. A decent cover can cost $200 to $1,000, but the quality is amazing.

On 99 Designs, you provide some basic information and start a contest. As a result, you often receive twenty to fifty unique designs within three to four days. I work with designers along the way, asking them to tweak the design. When the contest ends, you pick the finalists. Then you have four days to choose one and get the cover right.

Try it once. You just might be amazed at the results.

I'm writing this in mid-June. My eBay book sales have been sluggish for the last month. Then, one day, I noticed several regular sellers in my category switched out their covers and made some headway on the charts, so I gave it a shot, and sure enough, it gave a number of my titles a nice boost in sales.

Preview your book

At the bottom of the first page, you can preview your book as it will look on Kindle and Kindle for PC.

Do it. Do it more than once.

I always download a copy of my book to my Kindle Fire every few days as I write it. That way, I can read it in the format readers will see.

This does two things:

1. It forces me to read the book the way most of my readers will.
2. It alerts me to any formatting errors to get them corrected before publication.

Whatever you do, don't publish your book with formatting errors. Readers will blast you with terrible reviews and tank your book.

Verify rights and set price

At the top of the second page, you are asked to verify your publishing rights. Normally, if you are the author, just click worldwide and let her go. If there is a reason you can only publish your book in certain markets, select those areas, and you're ready to roll.

Pricing is a sensitive area for most authors. Of course, we all want to get as much money as possible for our books, but you must balance that with what readers are willing to pay.

Amazon gives you some guidance based on the royalties they pay.

- Books priced between 99 cents and $2.98 pay the author a 35 percent royalty.
- Books priced between $2.99 and $9.99 pay the author a 70 percent royalty.
- Books priced from $10.00 to $200.00 (the maximum amount you can charge on Kindle) pay a 35 percent royalty.

This tells us Amazon feels the sweet spot for Kindle books is between $2.99 and $9.99. We know this because this is where Amazon pays authors the highest royalties.

From my personal experience, books priced at $2.99 sell really well. At $3.99, you will encounter resistance, depending on how long your book is and what the competition charges. Your book may still sell okay at $4.99 and $5.99. Anything over $5.99 will hit some

Sell It Online

serious resistance unless you are a celebrity or a big-name author.

A lot of authors sell their books for 99 cents. That makes it tough to make money. A 99-cent book pays 35 percent royalties. That means you make 35 cents for each copy sold. To make ten bucks, you need to sell thirty books, whereas, at $2.99, you only need to sell five books to make that same ten bucks.

That's not to say 99 cents is a bad pricing strategy. I use it when my sales are weak. For example, one of my titles ran out of steam last month. I priced it at 99 cents for three weeks to pick up momentum. It sold 100 copies at 99 cents, and since I returned the price to $2.99 this month, it is on course to sell 60 copies.

After entering your price, check the box at the bottom asking you to confirm rights, and click publish.

In less than twelve hours, you will be a published writer.

I've published my book. Now what?

That's a good question.

The first thing you want to do is download a copy and read it over. Check for formatting issues, typos, and grammatical errors. This is your last chance to change things before it goes live to readers.

If you're happy with everything, schedule your free promo days (if you enrolled your book in KDP). Every author has a different strategy for this. My thought is five days work best for new authors. It gives you time to build momentum. Normally, your first few days will be slow, but people will start downloading more copies as time passes.

Getting Reviews

Another magical thing begins around day three of your free giveaway; you start getting reviews. I read somewhere you average one review for every thousand copies downloaded or sold. That means if you get 5,000 free downloads, you can figure on getting five reviews. Sometimes you get more. Sometimes you can have a great giveaway and not get any reviews. Don't sweat it. It happens.

I was really worried `about my first few books. Reviews were scarce, and everybody said, "You can't sell books without reviews." So, I finally asked some friends to review my book. Some did, some didn't, but most of those reviews weren't very helpful. Friends tend to write one or two-line reviews that go something like this, "A great read. I really liked it."

Unfortunately, readers like reviews that have a little meat to them. They want to know why the reviewer liked or didn't like the book. They want to know why the reviewer found your book useful or entertaining.

Don't worry. Those reviews will come. Sixty books, and nearly twelve years later, I have over 1,000 reviews. Many of them are really great four and five-star reviews. A few of them are one and two-star reviews. Good reviews happen, and so do bad reviews. All of them can help sell your books.

I only read the one and two-star reviews. They often tell me everything I need to know. It's a given that four and five-star reviews will be positive, so why waste time reading them.

Kindle Book Marketing 101

There's a lot of advice out there about how to market your book. I'm not a big believer in any of it.

I've sold thousands of books in the last year without doing anything other than optimizing my Amazon profile. So, I will show you how to maximize your profile on Amazon, and then I will refer you to a few books on advanced marketing techniques.

Book Description

We've already talked about your book description.

You need to understand that your book description is a work in progress. Keep tweaking it. Test different versions until you get the best description you can.

Never be satisfied until you get the sales you want. Instead, try writing a description of your book; introduce your characters; offer a book summary; lead with complimentary reviews; as you become better known, talk more about yourself.

The thing is, you never know what's going to attract people's attention until you give it a shot.

Kindle Countdown Deals

Kindle offers several marketing programs to help authors get the word out about their books and sell more copies.

The first program is KDP Free Days. I already talked about them earlier in this book. Every ninety days, you have the opportunity to give your book away for five days, or you can run a Kindle Countdown Deal for seven days.

KDP-free days can be used to launch a new book or launch an unknown writer's career. Amazon gives you five free days every ninety-day period you're enrolled in KDP. You can give your book away five days in a row, for five separate days, one two-day period, and one three-day period. How you choose to use them is entirely up to you.

If you do an internet search, you'll hear a lot of talk about how KDP Free Days don't work anymore. That may be true. Then again, it may not. It depends upon you and your book. It's all about how you choose to market your book. There are still a lot of authors who've launched a successful book or career using KDP Free Days.

Kindle Countdown Deals allow authors to promote their books by lowering the price for a limited period.

For every ninety days, your book is enrolled in KDP; you can run a Countdown Deal or use KDP Free Days (not both). Authors can promote discounted prices with the Countdown Deal for as little as one hour, up to seven days. You can choose to set your books at 99¢ for the entire promo, or you can set in on a sliding scale where it moves up in price after a certain period. Discount pricing depends upon the regular price of your book. The good thing for authors is even though you set your price below $2.99, Amazon pays you a 70 percent royalty.

Each time a reader clicks on your book description Amazon shows the promotional price beside a Countdown timer that lets buyers know how much time is left on the offer. Amazon also has a special landing page for Countdown Deals, so readers can only search among those books.

Amazon has another promo for authors enrolled in KDP. It's called Kindle Unlimited, and it lets subscribers read an unlimited number of books for only $9.99 per month. You get paid each time a reader selects your book. The current rate paid to authors varies based on how much money Amazon has stashed into its secret fund. (Most recently, the payout averages 45 to 50 cents per hundred pages read)

Another program lets authors set their books up for pre-order. The neat thing with this program is all the sales go live on the day your book launches, so if you score enough pre-orders, you can rocket your book up the charts from day 1.

Amazon Author Central

Amazon created Author Central as an area for writers to showcase information about themselves and their works.

We know that if people like your writing style or message, they will want to know more about you. What you look like? How you got started writing? Where you live, and what other books you've published.

To claim your Author Central page, visit the following link:

https://authorcentral.amazon.com/gp/home?ie=UTF8&pn=irid37437482

Upload an author biography to introduce yourself. Add a picture so readers can look at your bright and smiling face. Author Central allows you to collect all your books in one place so readers can browse through them.

Each time you publish a new book, click on Add Book to add your latest tile to your list of books.

Another interesting option Amazon offers is linking your blog and Twitter account to your Author Central Account. When you do this, your most recent tweet and highlights from your three most recent blog posts show up. Talk about a great way to engage your readers, and get them to follow you.

You also have a spot to upload book trailers or promotional videos. If you're photogenic or good with video, you could create a series of videos to allow readers to learn more about you and your books.

Many people link their books to Facebook or website, but a link to Author Central might pay off better in the long run. Not only does it introduce readers to you, but it also gives you a great opportunity to sell more of your books.

Final Thoughts

Writing an eBook is a great way to make some extra money.

Don't let the hype fool you. One book isn't going to make you rich. But, over time, if it is well written and on a popular topic, it can bring you several hundred dollars per month in royalties.

The real magic starts when you have a backlist of ten to twenty books in a related field. When this happens, people will read one of your books, and if they like it, chances are they will pick up one or two more. Some of them may even read the entire series.

If you want to make money writing, my best advice is to look at each book as a stepping stone to a larger audience and increased sales.

Finally, most of the information I shared with you focused on optimizing your Amazon profile to increase book sales. Many authors insist a strong author platform is your best marketing tool.

They think you need an author website, a blog, and at the minimum, a Facebook and Twitter account.

For more information on building an author platform, you can check out the following books:

- *Building Your Fanbase: A From Scratch Guide for Indie Authors*, by Duolit and Shannon O'Neil.
- *Blog It! The Author's Guide to Building a Successful Online Brand*, by Molly Greene
- *Book Marketing Basics: How to Use Facebook, Twitter, Blogging, and Email Marketing to Connect With Readers*, by Duolit.
- *Giving the Bird: The Indie Author's Guide to Twitter*, by Benjamin Wallace.

- *How to market a Book, by Joanna Penn.*

Blogging

Running a blog can be the most fun you ever have while working, but make no doubt about it—it's hard work.

Here are some of the things it takes to be a successful blogger:

1. **A Great Topic**. The success of your blog ultimately comes down to the topic you pick—the more people interested in it, the larger your potential audience.
2. **Interesting Content**. There are millions of different blogs out there. People will only read yours if you can supply a steady stream of interesting content.
3. **Writing Skills**. You don't have to be another Hemingway or Faulkner, but you need to know how to string a few sentences together. You should also know the ins and outs of your word processor, including how to use spellcheck and clean up those squiggly green lines the grammar checker shows.
4. **Ability to consistently post content**. To be a successful blogger, you must consistently create and post new content. Unfortunately, too many

blogs are unsuccessful, fade away, and die because the owner fails to provide new content.

5. **Unique content**. Not only do you have to provide well-written, interesting content, but it also needs to be unique. If you want to build an audience, you have to provide unique new content before others do.
6. **Video, audio, and photo skills**. People expect more than words. So you need to provide a variety of content, including videos, photos, and audio recordings.
7. **Basic SEO Skills**. You need to be able to identify keywords and know how to write your blog posts and titles so they will be optimized for Search Engine Optimization. In addition, you need to organize your content, so it will be easy for search engines to find and identify your content.
8. **Monetization skills**. At some point, you will want your blog to make money. To do that, you need to find different ways to monetize it, either by selling ads on your site or content such as eBooks or other information products.
9. **Stick-to-it-iveness**. What do I mean by this? You need to stick with it, even when you're sure no one is looking at your content. You need to keep posting great content, even when it means

missing a golf game, a movie, or special time with your family.

Some blogs take right off. But, more often, it will take time for your blog to gain momentum and pick up followers. That's why choosing a popular topic you are passionate about is important. You'll spend a lot of time with your blog, so make sure you enjoy your topic.

Choosing your blog topic

More than anything else, the topic you choose to blog about will determine your success.

In my experience, these are the most popular topics people tune into:

- Love
- Money
- Celebrity gossip
- Mom info
- Look good
- Feel good
- Hobbies
- Weight loss

Choosing any of these topics will help you draw more traffic right out of the box.

To become successful, you need to focus on just one small section of a topic, not the entire topic. Here's what I mean. There are probably a million blogs about how to make money online. If you choose to blog about making money online, your message will get lost in the blogosphere.

If you narrow your blog topic down and instead concentrate on making money selling textbooks on Amazon, your audience will be much smaller, but it will also be more focused. Everyone who visits your site will be interested in that topic. If you provide relevant content, they will keep returning to your blog.

Weight loss is another one of those subjects everybody and their brother has a blog or a website about. That doesn't mean you can't launch a successful weight-loss blog. It means you need to develop your niche. Focus on a theme. Weight Loss for Men over Fifty, Tone Your Thighs and Firm Your Buttocks, How to Lose Weight After Pregnancy.

The narrower your niche, the easier it will be to provide quality content relevant to your audience.

Set up your blog

Many blogging platforms are available: Blogger, Word Press, Tumblr, and Typepad. Any of them will work for your new blog.

The two most popular options are Blogger and Word Press. They offer more flexibility and control over your blog.

I prefer Blogger. It's easy to use. It offers a good variety of themes and layouts and is easy to monetize (they have a built-in option to add Google AdSense). In addition, you can assign a custom URL to your blog, giving it a more professional look and feel.

Other people swear by Word Press. It offers more features than Blogger and is served on an independent platform, so you have total control over your blog. In addition, it has thousands of pre-made themes you can download and apply to your blog, allowing you to use a custom URL.

The choice ultimately comes down to which you prefer. Either one will do a great job for you.

What type of content should you provide?

Content is king on your blog.

You must consistently provide great content that educates, informs, and entertains your audience. If your content is bad, it doesn't matter how many readers you draw to your blog; they won't bookmark your site and return for another serving.

With that said, what kind of content should you provide?

Here is a short list of the types of posts you should try to provide:

Lists. People go goo-goo ga-ga over lists. These are some of the most popular blog posts you can write. It can be as simple as a list of the top ten ways to save money on Wi-Fi or twenty-five ways to lose stubborn belly fat.

Something about a list makes people want to take a peek and see what they're missing. Hint: Include a number in the title, and the readership will triple. I don't know what it is, but including a number in your title reels people in.

Short informational posts. These are some of the easiest posts you will write. They should be between 300 to 500 words and focused on a single topic. Make it informative but light and easy to read.

Write three or four of these posts every month. They're a quick, easy way to connect with your audience.

Wrap up or overview post. You pick a topic and curate content on it in a wrap-up post. For example, if I was publishing a celebrity blog, I might write about celebrity baby bumps. I could do a review piece highlighting content hosted on other blogs or news magazines in the past week or month.

This post will take a little longer to put together because you need to gather links and write a short article that ties them all together. Review posts offer an easy way to add videos to your blog. Search YouTube for related videos, write a brief comment connecting it to your post, and embed the video. (Warning: Blogger will take down many videos, probably because of possible copyright infringement issues.)

Depending upon your subject, you can do one of these posts every week, two weeks, or month. It's the type of post people will keep coming back for if you can provide them with good useful links.

Tell a story. Everybody loves to hear a good story. At least once a month, you should share a story with your audience. It doesn't have to be long. 250 to 500 words are fine. It can be about something that happened to you, a historical event, or something happening in the news. Be sure to keep it light and entertaining.

Informational post. These are the pillar of your blog. They offer an in-depth look at one particular aspect of your topic and can run anywhere between 1500 to 3500 words depending upon the subject.

For these posts to be effective, they need to contain unique and useful information. In addition, they should contain links to outside sources, videos, and other people's blogs.

The easiest way to discover a relevant topic is to Google "hot topics in *****." The search results should return things your audience is interested in right now. So pick one, and give your audience the answers they need to form an opinion.

Interview someone in your field. One of the easiest ways to become an authority figure is to be seen in the company of people who already have that authority. Interviewing a celebrity or authority figure is a great way to piggyback off their fame.

Getting started is easier than you think. If you want to interview another blogger, check out their contact page and drop them an email. Keep it short and to the point. Give them a link to your blog, and explain what you want to do.

You can do the same thing with the author of a book concerning your blog topic. Contact the author and let them know you are reviewing their book and you would like to include a sidebar about them. Most authors will be glad to answer a few questions and even supply a current photo you can publish with the interview. Make it a win-win for both of you.

Whenever I've been interviewed or conducted an interview, we normally swap questions and answers by email and follow up with a short phone call to answer any lingering questions the interviewer might have.

How-to posts. People love how-to posts. Depending on what you are trying to explain, they can be as short as one hundred words or as long as several thousand words.

How-to posts are an excellent opportunity to add video, especially if it's a hands-on project. Let me give you an example: My wife broke the "H" key on her computer. She purchased the repair kit online for $7.00 but didn't know how to install it. So along comes YouTube to the rescue with a detailed video showing how to replace a computer key.

You could create videos or find a series on YouTube and present links to them to help solve your reader's problems.

Posting schedule

Search engines love websites that consistently add new and unique content. The more often you add content, the more often they send their spiders out to search for it.

As a new blogger, your first goal should be to post ten or fifteen great articles as quickly as possible. Content is the most important thing at this point. You want to have enough articles on your blog to convince your audience that you can deliver the info they want.

Once you've posted your initial articles, it's time to develop a regular blogging schedule.

One or two weekly posts are fine, especially if you deliver solid content. But shake them up a bit. Offer some informational posts, short posts, a how-to, an interview, and a wrap-up. People come in different flavors, and you can never be sure which type of post they will find more enjoyable.

Statistical tracking

To know where you're going, you need to know where you've been.

Blogging is sort of like taking a trip. We always watched the odometer to determine how far we traveled on vacation as kids. A statistical tracker does the same thing for your blog. It lets you see how much traffic your blog receives. What I like about blogger is it has a blog stats feature built into the control panel. I can tell at a glance what my top blog posts were for the day, week, or all time; where the traffic came from; what operating system readers used; and the keywords they searched on to bring them there.

For more detailed information, you can install Google Analytics on your blog. It's easy to use. You just need to sign up for the service (It's free) and copy the tracking code into your posts. Google Analytics gives you awesome details about your website visitors, down to which pages they entered and exited your blog from and how long they spent viewing each post.

My recommendation is to spend an hour every week or two reviewing your stats. It will give you great insight into your visitors and where they spend their time on your blog. Of course, the answer might be different than what you expect. You never know until you check.

Monetizing your blog

There are numerous ways to monetize your blog.

The most popular choice is Google AdSense. AdSense lets you place display and text ads on your blog strategically. Then, each time one of your readers clicks on an ad, Google pays you a percentage of the revenue they earned from it.

Over time Google gets good at matching ads to your website, so more people will click on them. The bad part is you aren't going to make a lot of money on AdSense until you start to have some good traffic numbers. For example, my QC Jobs website averaged 5,000 to 6,000 visitors per month. AdSense hovered around $150 to $200 per month.

Depending on your content, you can find many affiliate programs that might fit in. For example, adult Friend Finder has a good-paying affiliate program if you have a dating site. On the other hand, if your blog focuses on a profession or technical area, you might look at Indeed and Simply Hired job links.

Some of the bigger affiliate sites are Commission Junction and Link Share. They offer programs from some of America's largest businesses. Be aware that most advertisers reserve the right to accept or reject your website. You will not be accepted if your content or visitor count doesn't mesh with their minimum requirements. Keep trying; eventually, you should find many attractive offers for your audience.

eBay has a good-paying affiliate program if you can get accepted. I've tried several different websites and have been rejected for all of them. Despite that, I still have eBay ads on my site. It's just that Google AdSense serves them up.

Amazon Affiliates is another program used by a lot of bloggers. With Amazon, you can use their widgets to build an entire store full of products targeted to your niche, or you can select individual items. The cool thing here is if you have a big enough audience, you could review a book or movie and link to it with your Amazon Affiliate account. Then, each time one of your readers purchases it, you would receive a cut of the profits.

Finally, you can sell individual ad spots on your blog. Some blogs have large banner ads. Others offer smaller ads they label as sponsors. Either way allows you to pick up a few extra bucks.

Final wrap up

Blogging is a fun way to reach out to like-minded people and have the opportunity to make some extra money at the same time. Just remember, it's not a sure thing, and it's not a get-rich-quick scheme. You need to put in the time and build an audience.

Content is king. If you plan on being a successful blogger, you must provide many unique, entertaining content.

Online Courses & Coaching

Have you ever thought life would be much easier if someone was there to help you through the rough spots? Someone you could bounce your ideas off? Someone who could help you tame the thoughts running wild in your head?

That's what a coach does. She's the one who listens to what you have to say. She asks you questions to help you clarify your goals, then works with you to develop a plan to help you move from point A to Point B.

She often does it all through a series of internet coaching sessions.

Other coaches conduct internet training classes to help people develop all sorts of skills, including,

1. Train people how to sell on eBay
2. Teach people how to manage small business finances with QuickBooks
3. Help people develop a personalized weight loss program
4. Show people how to plan for a career change, get ready for retirement, or how to sell their house in today's market

You name it, and somebody's running an online training class to help people solve their problems.

This section will show you how to get started with this career opportunity.

Getting Started

Getting started in online coaching is often as easy as hanging your shingle out and screaming here I am – Expert for hire!

The great thing about the coaching business is that no licenses or certifications are required to get started. Unfortunately, the bad thing about the coaching business is that no licenses or certifications are necessary.

Do you see the Catch 22?

There are no legal or training barriers to keep you from getting started, but you will be in a business environment surrounded by many quacks and charlatans.

So how do you stand out from the crowd?

1. It would help if you were an expert in your field because you need to know what you're talking about. That means you need to walk the walk and talk the talk.

2. While it's not required, a bachelor's degree or advanced degree in the field you want to coach will add credibility.
3. A certificate in coaching can help if it's from a good training program.
4. You need to keep up with the latest coaching methods and delivery systems.

The best coaches are the ones who've been working in a particular field for their entire life. They have the practical experience people want to learn.

If you don't have practical experience, the next best thing is academic training. If you have an MBA in online marketing, you have the knowledge people need to build their web-based businesses.

A quick Google search will return plenty of online certification programs. Many offer solid training that will give you a head start at launching your online coaching business. Others are certificate mills designed to make money rather than show you how to get started. Perform your *due diligence* before enrolling in any program.

Online coaching is a business. To be successful, you need to understand how other successful coaches conduct their business. In addition, you need to keep up with the latest internet technologies, such as Skype and GoToMeeting.

What does a coach do?

Before you get started, you need to know what a coach does.

Many people think a coach is like a teacher. However, they are more like a mentor.

Here's the difference: A teacher spoon-feeds you knowledge and tells you how to do something. A coach helps you clarify your goals and create an action plan for moving from Point A to Point B. Once the action plan is decided upon, the coach ensures that the client acts upon it.

Listening is one of the most important skills you are going to need. Your job is to get your client talking and help them to see themselves more clearly. You ask questions and challenge clients to expand upon their ideas.

You need to get people thinking about where they are and what it will take to get them where they want to be.

If you're a career coach and your client wants to make a career change, you need to help them look at the big picture. That means you need to help them see where they are today. Next, you need to help them determine what skills they need to succeed in a new career. After that, help them identify their current skills, what skills they need to develop, and if they need to add any training or certification programs to get there.

The final step is to help your client develop an action plan for achieving their goal. Then, you need to help them lay out the steps and hold them accountable for moving from Point A to Point B.

Couldn't your client do the same thing for themselves?

Your clients could do the same thing themselves, but think about yourself or some of the people you know.

It's easy to say so and so should have done… But it's harder to make a decision when it comes to yourself. Sometimes we're too hard on ourselves; sometimes, we're too easy on ourselves. It's hard to see the big picture when talking about yourself. That's why so many people turn to coaches. They need help to make important changes in their life. But, more importantly, they need someone to make them accountable for those changes.

Online training

Online training is similar to coaching, except you deliver a compact solution to your student's problems.

Most online training classes are tightly focused. They teach one skill. Examples are:

- How to use QuickBooks in your small construction business
- How to sell collectibles on eBay
- Selling on eBay for seniors
- Wedding cake decorating
- How to start a window-washing business

Notice how focused each of the classes is. People want to learn specific skills to help them solve a problem TODAY.

Your class can help them make money or learn a life skill. For example, you could focus your class on assisting new mothers to slim down after having a baby. Other courses teach adult children how to care for aging parents who've moved back into their homes.

You name a topic, and thousands of people will be interested in learning about it.

I've got an idea, how do I deliver it

Often getting an idea for a training class is easy. However, figuring out how to deliver it can be a challenge.

Keep in mind everyone learns differently and at a different pace.

Some people are visual.

They need to see something to be able to do it. So, to teach these people, you will need to train them in person or deliver their training through a series of videos.

Other people learn by reading.

This group would benefit from an online course where most of the information is delivered in text and charts. In this situation, you would provide the information through an online platform or weekly emails. You could give assignments and quizzes to keep the class interactive. You would need to follow up with students by email or phone if necessary.

Webinars are an easy way to deliver online training.

GoToMeeting is one of many providers offering solutions for online training sessions. I have attended many seminars delivered on their platform. Most last from forty-five minutes to an hour and a half.

You can let students watch your talk; you can use a whiteboard system or show PowerPoint slides to enhance your talk. The program also lets presenters provide PDFs of the presentation that attendees can print to follow along or keep for future reference.

Putting it all together

Online training classes are great for delivering focused training to your clients.

To get started, you need to decide your delivery method. Earlier, we discussed using an online teaching platform, email courses, and webinars.

After deciding on a delivery method for your training class, you must develop your material.

Most online training classes run from four to six weeks. They last approximately forty-five minutes to an hour per session. So you want to keep them short and focused.

Tailor your presentation to the subject you are teaching. For example, suppose you're conducting an online review for bankruptcy lawyers. In that case, your material will be at a higher level than a class presented to teenage moms on how to breastfeed their new babies.

Most trainers teach at the eighth-grade level. That way, they know most of their students will understand the material they are presenting.

You also want to think about your style. For example, suppose you are photogenic and enjoy being in front of people. In that case, you may want to conduct in-person seminars and then sell videos of them as your online training class.

This is becoming increasingly popular as the price of in-person seminars increases.

One person who does this is Lynn Dralle, who bills herself as the Queen of Auctions. She has written several books on eBay auctions and conducts live training sessions. In addition, she recorded her 2008 Boot Camp on eBay selling and is offering it as Boot Camp in a Box for $997 a pop.

Think about it. You teach a weekend seminar once, at $2500 or more a head; you record it and sell it for years at a thousand dollars a crack.

What could be better than that?

What about training books?

We already talked about Kindle books.

What if you create a series of short training books and sell them from your website—charging $39.00 to $249.00 each, depending upon the information you have in them.

In this case, your $2.99 Kindle book could be the bait to take people to your more focused and expensive training classes.

To do this properly, you need a website. You also need to build an authority platform around yourself and your products. One Kindle author doing a great job of this is Steve Scott.

Steve has an authority website he encourages his Kindle readers to visit for a free eBook. After he has you on his email list, he gets back to you every few weeks with info on his new books as they are released or about any sales he offers. You can visit Steve at the Steve Scott site to see what he is doing.

Final wrap up

Think outside of the box!

Determine what you are good at. Then, create a niche where you can become an expert. Write books. Create short reports. Make videos and audiotapes of you presenting your material.

Most importantly, build a website or blog that can be a home base for your consulting and training activities.

Remember, all good things take time. Grow your business slowly. Add activities that enhance your business and grow your authority in your niche.

If you plan to do several distinct things, create a separate identity and website for each activity.

Doing too many things will confuse your audience and cost you sales.

Good luck and great success in your new business.

Remember, every success starts by taking the first step. After that, a series of baby steps will move you along your path.

What's next?

Congratulations! You've made your way through the entire book!

Hopefully, it got your creative juices flowing, and you've come up with some great ideas about what you can sell online. But, whatever you decide, I urge you to get started as soon as possible. So often, when people read a book like this, they want to get started, but they determine they should wait...

...wait until they have more money to put into it.

...wait until they have more time...

...wait until...

You get the idea. Often it is fear of failure that keeps us from trying. We want to get started, but we're afraid to tell friends or loved ones what we're doing because we're unsure what they will say.

When I wrote my first book, I didn't tell anyone about it, not my wife, kids, or friends.

A month later, when it hit number one in the eBay category on Amazon, I decided it was time. So I sat down with my wife and told her, "I've got something I should tell you...."

I'm saying, don't let fear of failure hold you back. Hundreds of thousands of people are making a full or part-time income selling online. You can, too, if only you dare to try.

....

Sell It Online

CPSIA information can be obtained
at www.ICGtesting.com
Printed in the USA
LVHW021028030523
745986LV00020B/352